CATHERALL, E.

J/582.16

ST. AUSTELL M/L
Tel. 3348   7/83

FOWEY
Tel 2332 4/8

GW01549674

WITHDRAWN

Trees

Ed Catherall

Wayland

Young Scientist

Electric Power
Solar Power
Water Power
Wind Power

Hearing
Sight
Taste and Smell
Touch

Clocks and Time
Levers and Ramps
Magnets
Wheels

Trees
The Seashore
Energy for Life
Flowering Plants

First published in 1982 by Wayland Publishers Limited
49 Lansdowne Place, Hove, East Sussex BN3 1HF, England
© Copyright 1982 Wayland Publishers Limited
ISBN 0 85340 991 9

Illustrated and designed by David Anstey
Typeset by Tunbridge Wells Typesetting Services Ltd.
Printed in Italy by G. Canale & C.S.p.A, Turin

Contents

Chapter 1 Adopting a tree

Selecting your tree 4
Mapping your tree 5
Measuring your tree 6
Tree shapes 7
Exploring tree trunks 8
Making bark rubbings 9
Tree branches 10

Chapter 2 Leaves

Leaf arrangement 11
Exploring twigs 12
What is inside a bud? 13
Leaf shape 14
Making patterns with leaves 15
Leaf size and growth 16
Leaf damage 17
Leaves and water 18
Preserving leaves 19
Falling leaves 20

Chapter 3 Tree fruits

Tree flowers 21
Tree fruits and seeds 22
Fruit trees 23
Tree seeds 24

Chapter 4 Timber

Calculating the age of a tree 25
Exploring logs and timber 26
Timber from trees 27

Chapter 5 Plants and animals on trees

Exploring leaf litter 28
Plants growing under trees 29
Plants on trees 30
Animals on trees 31
Exploring rotten wood 32

Chapter 1 Adopting a tree

Selecting your tree

Find a tree that you can visit regularly.
What kind of tree have you chosen?
Is your tree an evergreen?
Why did you pick this tree?
Is this tree a common tree in your area?
Was your tree planted or was it naturally seeded?

What do you know about your tree before you begin to study it?
Where did you get this information from?
Is there anything dangerous about your tree?

Start an illustrated book or scrap book about your tree. In this book record everything that you can find out about your tree.

Compare your tree with other trees of the same kind. Try to find out how your tree is different from other trees.

Try to study your tree for a whole year. Call your book *A year in the life of a _____ tree.*

Perhaps you could present your finished book to your school library?

Mapping your tree

Make two maps of the area surrounding your tree. The first map should be a general map of the area. Make a second map, of the detail around your tree.

Carefully record the number of your paces between landmarks.
Measure the sheets of paper that you will use for your maps. How many paces do you need to fit on to each sheet of paper?
Select a suitable scale.
The scale for your general map could be one pace equals one mm.
For the detailed map, the scale could be one pace equals one cm.

Carefully draw both maps to scale. Mark on your general map the area covered by your detailed map.
Mark the north direction on both maps.
Measure one of your paces.
What is the actual scale of each map?
Record the scales on your maps.

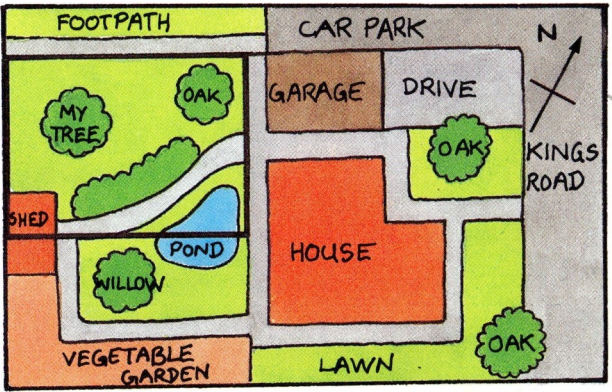

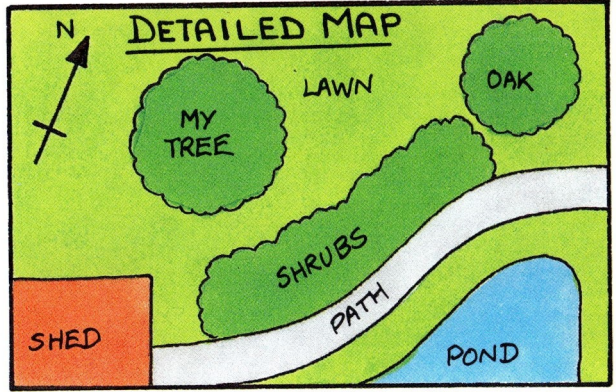

Measuring your tree

Ask a friend to help you measure your tree. Hold your ruler vertically at arm's length. Be sure to keep your ruler and arm still. Move back from your tree until your tree appears to be as long as your ruler. Stop and turn your ruler horizontally, so that the ruler starts at the trunk.
Ask your friend to pace out from your tree and stop her when she appears to be a ruler's length away from your tree.

How many paces did your friend take? How many paces is the height of your tree?
Measure the length of one of her paces.
How high is your tree?

Stand underneath your tree.
Look at the branches.

Mark on the ground how far the branches spread out.
Do the branches spread out an equal distance from the tree trunk?

Pace the distances from the trunk to several branch marks.
Measure the length of one of your paces.
How far out from the trunk do the branches spread?
Measure the diameter of the trunk of your tree.

Tree shapes

Many trees have a typical shape.
Draw pictures from memory of a
pine tree and a palm tree.
With practice, you could learn the
typical shapes of many different trees.

Is your tree trunk vertical?
Does your tree stand alone?
If your tree is near other trees, see
how these trees affect the shape of your tree.
Look at trees that grow close together.
What do you notice?

Does your tree stand near a building?
How does this building affect the shape of your tree?

Carefully measure your tree. (see page 6)
Do your tree's branches spread out
evenly around the trunk? (see page 6)
If they do not spread out evenly, can
you account for this? Has your tree ever been cut?
Many trees are affected by the prevailing wind.
Many trees grow towards the sun.

From which direction is it best to
draw your tree?
Carefully draw your tree to scale.
(see page 6)
Draw your tree during different
seasons of the year.
Date your tree drawings and put
them in your book.
Does your tree change shape?
Did your tree grow much in a year?

Summer Winter

Exploring tree trunks

What colour is your tree's bark?
Is the bark all the same colour?
Is the bark on the trunk the same as the bark on the large branches?

Look at the base of the trunk of your tree. Is the ground flat around the base of your tree?
Can you see any tree roots?
Are there hollows in your tree where rain could collect?

Foil collector
Plastic tub

Visit your tree after it has rained.
Is the bark of your tree wet?
Carefully feel the bark. Where is the bark wettest?
Can you see where the rain runs down the trunk of your tree?

Make a metal-foil rain collector.
Press the foil well into the trunk where you think the rain runs.
Collect the rainwater in a plastic tub.
Is this rainwater clear or dirty?
Can you work out why the rain runs down this side of the tree trunk? Does it always run down this side?
Look at other tree trunks to find out where the rain runs. Try to work out a rule about how rain runs down tree trunks.

Making bark rubbings

Feel the bark of your tree.
Are there places where the texture changes?
How large are the cracks in the bark of your tree?
How deep are these cracks?
Do these cracks form a pattern?
Is the bark of your tree dirty?

Tape several sheets of newspaper to your tree. The newspaper helps to prevent you from tearing your paper when you make a rubbing. The rougher the bark, the more sheets of newspaper you will need.

Tape a sheet of white paper over the newspaper.
Hold the paper steady with one hand while you rub the paper with a soft crayon. Rub the crayon evenly over the paper until you produce a good bark rubbing.

Make rubbings of different trees for comparison.

Does your tree shed its bark?
Never remove the bark from a living tree.
Never cut into the bark of a tree.
Look at trunks of trees for wounds.
What caused these wounds?
Are there any tree vandals in your area?

Tree branches

Do the branches of your tree grow upward, downward, or horizontally? Do all the branches of your tree grow in the same direction? Do the branches grow out evenly from the trunk? (see page 6)

Stand back from your tree. Which is the largest branch? How long is this branch? (see page 6) Is the longest branch also the thickest branch? At what height does this branch start growing out from the trunk?

Look carefully at how your branches divide. Do they always divide into pairs? Does each branch of the pair grow to the same length?

Count the number of times one branch has divided. Do most divisions occur near the trunk?

Look at a large branch. Does the bark on the branch change as you go along the branch? What changes can you see? What do you think causes these changes?

Have any of your tree branches been cut or damaged?

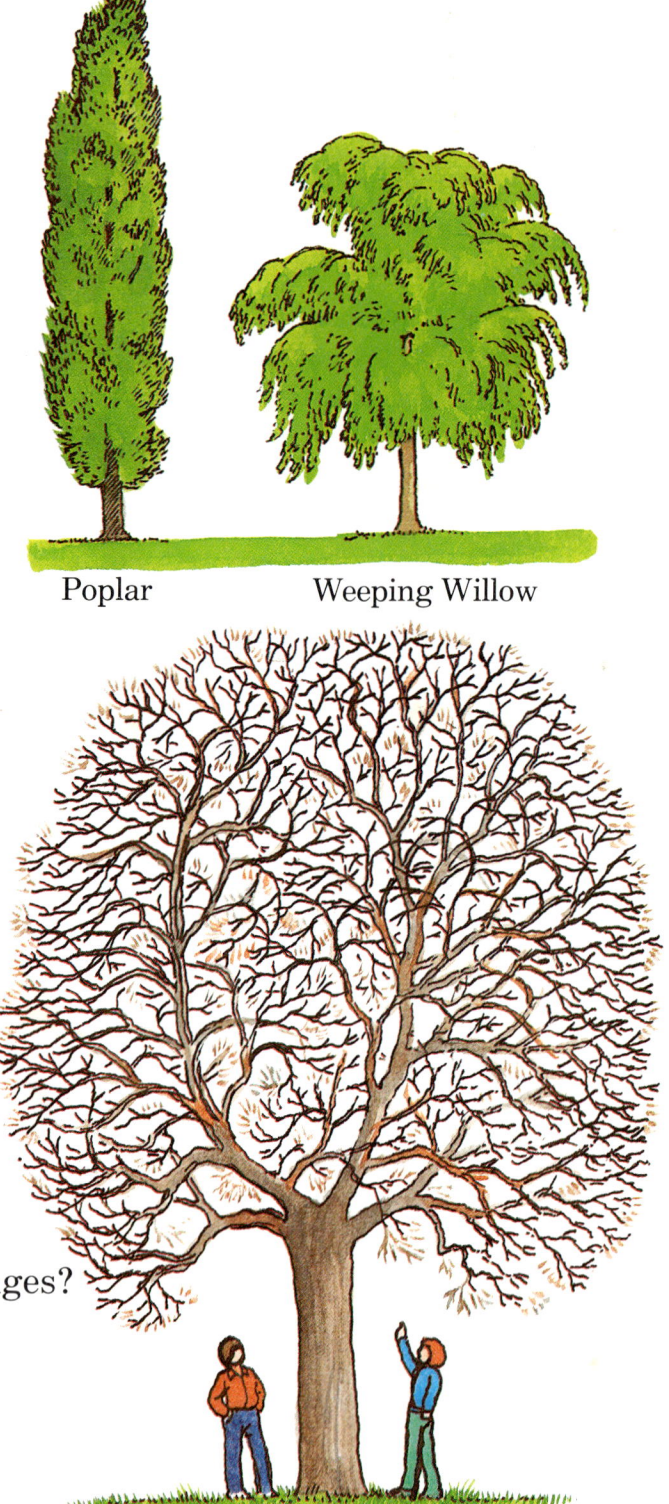

Poplar   Weeping Willow

Chapter 2 Leaves

Leaf arrangement

Look at the twigs on your tree.
Notice how the twigs branch.
Are all the twig branches the same?

Look at the leaves on your twig.
How are the leaves jointed to the twig?
How are the leaves arranged on
your twig?
Do the leaves follow a spiral
pattern up the twig? Do the leaves
wind clockwise?
How many leaves do you count
before you get to the leaf directly
above your starting leaf?
Do all the leaves follow the same pattern?
Draw a twig with its leaves.

Are there any twigs on your tree
that show different leaf
arrangements from the one that
you have drawn? Can you find a
reason for this? Is there any sign
of injury to this twig?

Look at twigs from other trees.
How is their leaf arrangement different from your tree?
Are there any trees with the same leaf pattern
as your tree?

Are there buds on your twig?
Where are the buds?
Do the buds follow the same pattern as the leaves?

Exploring twigs

Look at the twig of a deciduous tree in winter.
Are there any old leaves or fruits left on the twig?
Look for the buds on the twig.
Are the buds arranged on the twig in the same way as the leaves? (see page 11)

Find the scars on the twig left by the falling leaves.
What shape are these scars? Why are they this shape?
Are all these leaf scars the same size and shape?

Look for the set of girdle scars that are formed when the terminal bud bursts and the twig grows for a year.
Look along the twig for other sets of girdle scars. How many leaf scars are there between each set of girdle scars?
How many sets of girdle scars are on your twig?
How old is your twig?

Measure the distance between each set of girdle scars. Which was the best year for growth for your twig? Compare other twigs for that year's growth.
Do they all show the same growth for that year?
Can you find a very old, but short, twig?
Draw and label your twigs.

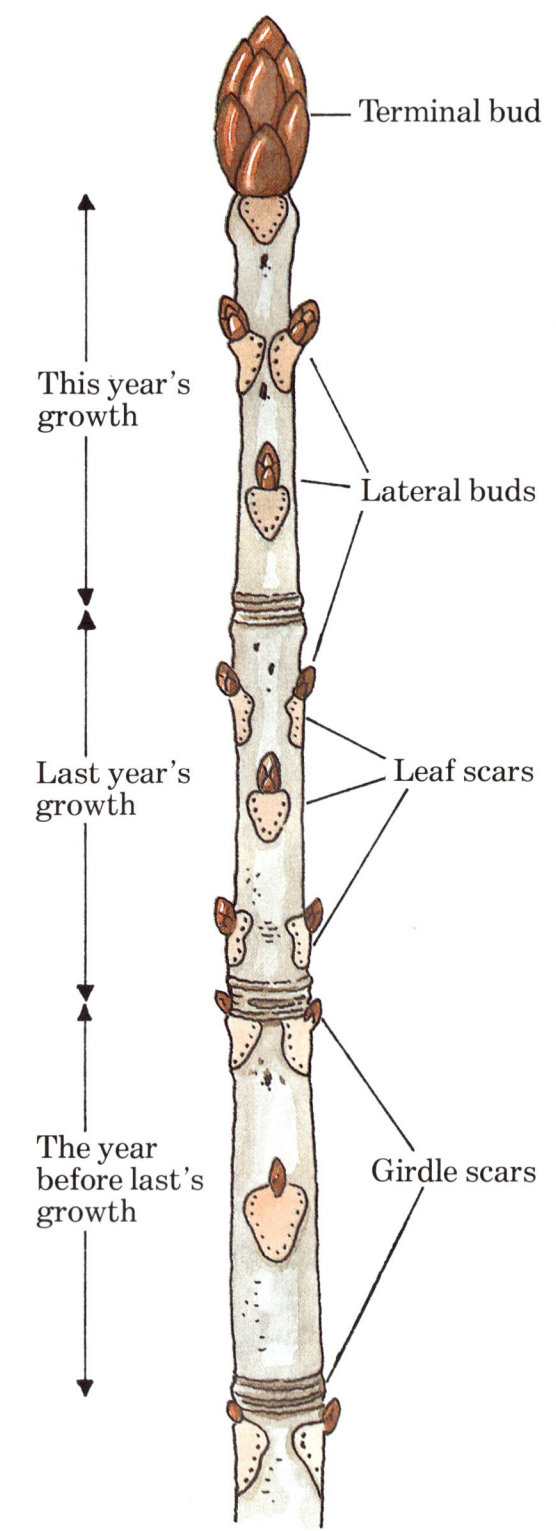

What is inside a bud?

Cabbages and lettuces are large terminal buds.
A Brussels sprout is a large lateral bud.
Cut a sprout in half to show the cross section.
Cut another sprout in half to show the radial section.
Draw your sprout sections.

Carefully remove the leaves from another sprout. How many leaves are in your sprout?

Cut from your tree a twig containing a large bud.
If the bud is sticky, wash it in surgical spirit.
Use tweezers and a pin to remove the leaves of your bud one at a time.
Tape the leaves from your bud on a card in the order in which you remove them.
Open other buds. How are they different?

When buds begin to open on your tree, cut off a twig.
Place the twig in water in a warm room.
Make drawings to show the stages of your bud opening.

Do all the buds open at the same time on your twig?
Do the big buds open first?
Is there a connection between the position of the bud on the twig and how soon it opens?

On which trees do the buds open first in your area?

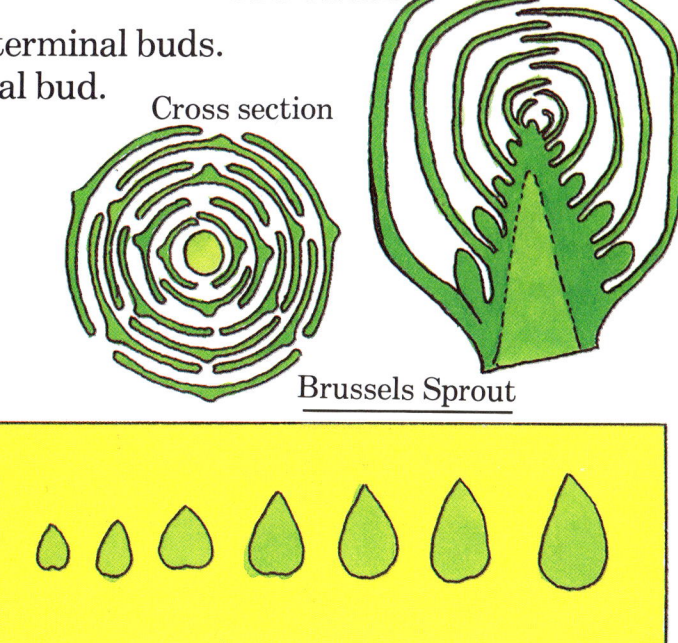

Cross section
Radial section
Brussels Sprout

Oak bud

Buds opening
March 4th
March 11th

Leaf shape

Look at the leaves of your tree.
What colours are the leaves?
How many different shades can you find?
Have all the leaves a similar shape?
Are the leaves simple or compound?
Where on the twigs are the largest leaves?
Do the largest leaves have the largest leaf stalks?

Remove a typical leaf from your tree.
Is the leaf dirty?
Compare the upper and lower surfaces.
How does the upper surface of the leaf compare with the lower surface?
On which surface is it easier to see the leaf veins?

A simple leaf

A compound leaf

Hold your leaf under a dripping tap.
What happens when a drop of water lands on the upper surface of the leaf?
What happens when a drop lands on the lower surface?

Is the edge of your leaf smooth?
Draw your leaf.
What do you notice about the branching of the veins on your leaf?

Making patterns with leaves

Put a leaf on a flat table.
Place a sheet of white paper over the leaf.
Hold the paper and leaf still with one hand while you rub the paper with a soft wax crayon.
Which makes the best rubbing, the upper or lower surface of your leaf?

Use a soft pencil to make another leaf rubbing.

Place a sheet of thin metal foil over your leaf. Hold the foil and leaf still with one hand while you rub the foil with a finger or a pencil.
Make metal imprints of different leaves.

Make an imprint by pressing your leaf into soft clay.

Make a creamy thick paint by mixing powder paint, water paste and water.

Foil
Leaf underneath

Carefully brush one surface of your leaf with your creamy paint.
Place your leaf, paint side down, on to absorbent paper, such as blotting paper.
Hold your leaf still with one hand while you rub the leaf with a finger to obtain a print.

Try printing with different colours.

Try printing on a piece of old cloth.
Use different leaves to vary your design.

Leaf size and growth

How long is your leaf?
How wide is your leaf?
If you multiply these two measurements, you will get some idea of the area of your leaf.
How thick is your leaf? Can you measure the leaf's thickness?

Clip a sheet of squared paper on to a smooth board.
Hold a leaf on your squared paper.
Be careful not to damage the leaf on your tree.
Hold the leaf still and carefully draw around the edge of the leaf.
If your leaf outline cuts through half or more than half a square count this square as a whole square.
If your leaf outline cuts through less than half a square do not count this square.
What is the area of one square on your paper? What is the area of your leaf?

Try to measure regularly the area of one young leaf. Be careful not to damage the leaf.
Count the squares covered by your leaf.
Calculate the increase in growth of your leaf.
Identify your leaf by tying thread around its stem.
Does your leaf grow at a steady rate?

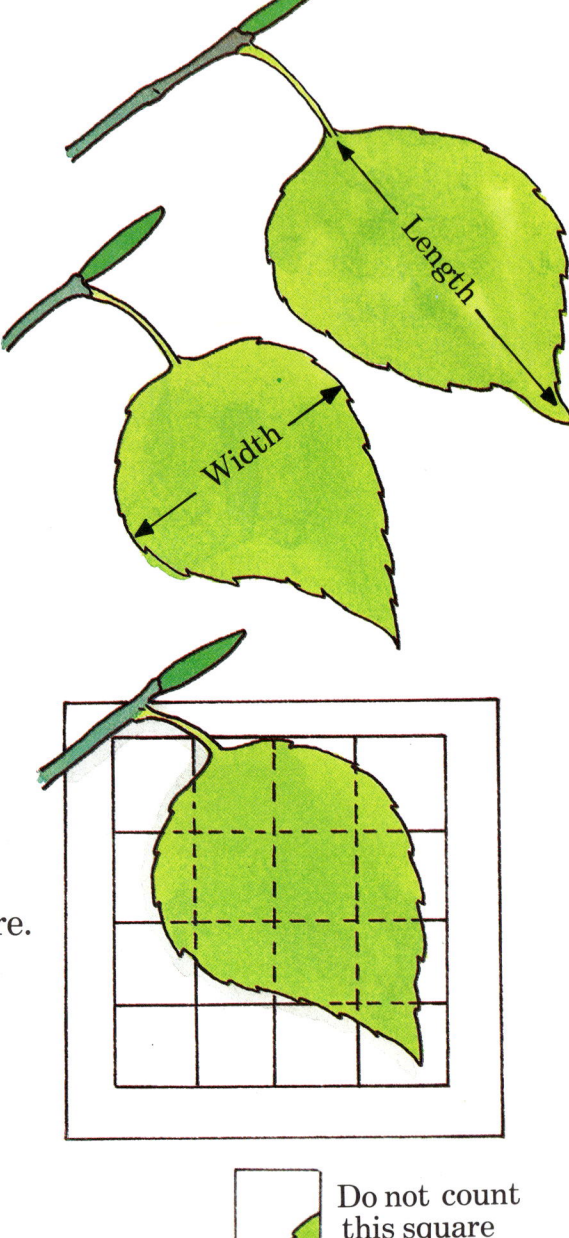

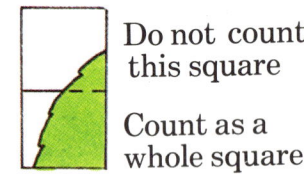

Do not count this square

Count as a whole square

Leaf damage

Are any leaves on your tree dying?
How can you tell that the leaf is dying?
What caused this leaf to die?

Are any of the leaves on your tree tightly curled? When you find a curled leaf, carefully uncurl it.
What is inside your curled leaf?

Some leaves have tunnels in them.
Leaf miner insects tunnel between the upper and lower surfaces of leaves. Find a leaf with a tunnel. Open the tunnel with a pin. Is the insect still inside?

Look for lumps on the upper or lower surface of leaves. These lumps could be leaf galls.
What shape are these galls?
What colour are these galls?
Galls are caused by young gall insects.

Look at the edges of your leaves.
Have any of the leaf edges been eaten?
Are there any leaves on your tree with holes in them? Use squared paper to find out how much of the leaf has been eaten.
(see page 16)

Has your tree more leaf damage than other trees? Which is the most common form of leaf damage in your area?
At what time of year is this damage done?

Leaves and water

On a dry day place a dry, clear plastic bag over some leaves on your tree.
Use tape to close the opening of your bag and tape the bag to the branch.
Make sure that there are no leaks.
Look at your bag every hour.
Is there moisture in the bag?
How much moisture can you collect in a day?
How many leaves are in the bag?
Try to estimate how many leaves there are on your tree.

How much water do you think your tree puts into the air each day?

Carefully cut from your tree a living twig with its leaves.
Make a hole in a tight-fitting jar lid.
Pass the twig through the hole.
Put water in the jar. Mark the water level. If the twig does not fill the hole, use clay or tape to stop the water from evaporating. Observe the water level daily. What happens?

Put a strong coloured food dye in the water.
After two days remove the twig. Make a cross section of the twig. Can you see the dye inside?

Preserving leaves

Are there any trees in your area with leaves that are not green?
What colour are the leaves?
What is the name of the tree?

Leaves of deciduous trees change colour before falling. Which deciduous tree in your area changes colour first?
Find a tree with leaves showing a range of colours.
How many different colours are the leaves?
Paint a picture of this tree.

Collect leaves showing a range of colours.
Arrange your leaves by order of colour.
Arrange your leaves to make a picture.

Place coloured leaves between sheets of newspaper or blotting paper.
Put books on the newspaper to keep the leaves flat.
Move the leaves every few days to stop them from sticking to the paper.
Dried leaves can be preserved by laminating them with clear plastic sheets.

Mix glycerine (glycerol) with an equal quantity of water.
Cut a living twig with its leaves from a tree.
Crush the end of the stem.
Place the crushed end of the stem in a jar containing your glycerine and water.
After one month remove the branch.
Display your preserved branch with dry wood or driftwood and dry woody fruits.

Falling leaves

All trees shed their leaves. Deciduous trees shed their leaves as a preparation for winter.
Try to catch a falling leaf.
Can you hear a leaf fall?
Which tree in your area starts to lose its leaves first?
Do the leaves of this tree change colour first?

Look at the first leaves to fall.
Do damaged leaves fall first?
Do the topmost leaves fall first?
Does the windy side of the tree lose its leaves first?
Do leaves fall on a still day?

Look at the leaves left on a twig.
Is there any pattern to leaf fall?
Do big leaves of one particular shape fall faster?
Must a leaf have changed colour before it falls?
Are falling leaves drier than those still on the tree?
How long does it take for your tree to lose all its leaves?

Carefully cut a living twig with its leaves from a tree.
Place the twig stem in water indoors in the warm.
Do the leaves still fall from your indoor twig?

Chapter 3 Tree fruits

Tree flowers

Is your tree old enough to bear flowers?
If your tree has flowers, when do the flowers come out?
Do the flowers come out before the leaves?

Look at a twig containing a flower.
Where on the twig is the flower? (see page 12)
Are the flowers arranged singly or in clusters? If the flowers are in clusters, are all the flowers in a cluster the same?
Do all the flowers in a cluster come out together?
How many flowers are there in a cluster?

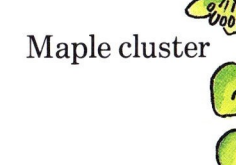
Maple cluster

Ash tree flowers

What colour are the flowers on your tree?
Are all the flowers on your tree the same?
Does your kind of tree have separate male and female flowers? Are they on the same tree? If they are on separate trees, how far apart are the two trees?

Carefully remove a flower from your tree.
Shake the flower on to white paper. Can you see any pollen on the paper?
Is the pollen of your tree carried by insects or by the wind?
Record the kinds of insects that visit the flowers on your tree.
Use a lens to look at the parts of your tree flower.
Draw a flower.
Cut a flower across to show its radial section. (see page 26)
Draw the cut surface.

Tree fruits and seeds

How big were the first fruits that dropped from your tree? What caused these fruits to fall early? Cut a young fruit in half in transverse section.
Cut a young fruit in half in radial section. Can you see a young seed inside?

Make a collection of the stages of growth of fruit from your tree. Draw the cut sections of the fruits.

How does a mature fruit get dispersed from your tree?

Make a collection of fruits from different trees. Which fruits are dispersed by the wind? Do these fruits have wings? What do these wings do? Release some winged fruits on a windy day. How do the fruits spin? How far do they travel? Which went furthest?

Which fruits and seeds are dispersed by bouncing and rolling? Drop these fruits and seeds from various heights on to different surfaces. What happens?

Have you ever seen an animal collect a tree fruit or a seed? Which fruits and seeds are carried by animals? Look on the ground for fruits and seeds that have been eaten by animals. Which fruits from trees are eaten by birds?

Transverse section

Radial section

Maple fruits

Nut eaten by squirrel

Fruit trees

The greatest dispersers of tree fruits are humans.
Which is your favourite fruit from a tree?
List all the tree fruits that you have eaten.
Nuts are fruits although you usually only eat the seed.

Which of all these fruits are grown locally?
Have you ever seen them growing?
How are they picked and sold?

Which fruits are transported a great distance to reach you?
Where are these fruits grown?
Which of these fruits were transported fresh?
How were these fruits transported?

Which tree fruits are preserved by freezing?
Which tree fruits are canned?
Which tree fruits are preserved in sugar?

Collect labels from different cans and packages of preserved tree fruits.
Arrange your label collection in your scrapbook.
Collect pictures of different fruit trees.
Find out how the fruit is picked from these trees.

Which citrus fruits do you know?
How are citrus fruits used?
Which is the strangest tree fruit that you know?

Tree seeds

Investigate the inside of tree fruits. By cutting, squashing or crushing tree fruit, find out how the seeds are arranged inside. Draw what you see. Record the number of seeds that you find inside each fruit.
Draw one of each seed.
Which fruit has the most seeds?
Which fruit has the least seeds?
Does any fruit have no seeds inside?

Do all fruits of the same kind have the same number of seeds inside? Do some varieties of apple have more seeds inside the fruit? Where are the seeds inside an orange?
Do all oranges have the same number of seeds inside them? Can you find seedless oranges? Where did the seedless oranges come from?

Plant seeds from all kinds of trees. Which seeds grow?
Some tree seeds are very difficult to grow. Plant the seeds from apples and oranges indoors.
Plant seeds from your tree.

Make drawings of your seedlings at regular intervals to show their growth.

Coconut seed

Oak seedling

Chapter 4 Timber

Calculating the age of a tree

Find a cut tree trunk or large log.
Was the tree cut recently?
How can you tell?
What tool do you think was used to cut down the tree?

Look at the cut end of your tree or log.
This is a transverse section.
Measure the thickness of the bark.
Explore the cut surface with a lens.
Find where the sapwood starts.
The sapwood is lighter in colour than the central heartwood.
How thick is the sapwood layer?
How thick is the heartwood layer?
Draw your log or tree section.

Deciduous trees form new wood only in spring and summer. Spring wood is lighter in colour than summer wood.
These differences can be seen as annual rings.
A new ring is formed each year.
Count the number of rings on the cut surface.
Trees usually take five years to form the central heartwood so add five years to the age of the tree.
Look at the width of different annual rings.
Which years were good growing years?
By looking at particular annual rings can you tell anything about the weather that year?
How could you check your guesses?

Exploring logs and timber

Look at the transverse section of a log.
Ask an adult to help you saw your log across its diameter.
Identify the layers in your radial section. Draw your log and label the layers.

Ask an adult to help you saw your log to make a tangential section.
What layers have you cut through?
Draw your tangential section to show the pattern.

Find a log with a branch growing out of the side.
Ask an adult to help you saw your log in transverse or radial section through where the branch starts.
What kind of section of the branch do you get?
Can you see where the branch starts from the trunk of the tree?
Notice how the branch makes a knot in the wood. Draw a section showing the branch.

Investigate pieces of timber and wooden furniture.
Try to identify the sections on the face of the timber.
Are there knots or knot holes in the timber?

Look for beautiful wood veneers. What colours can you see in the veneer? Find out the names of the trees that produce these veneers?

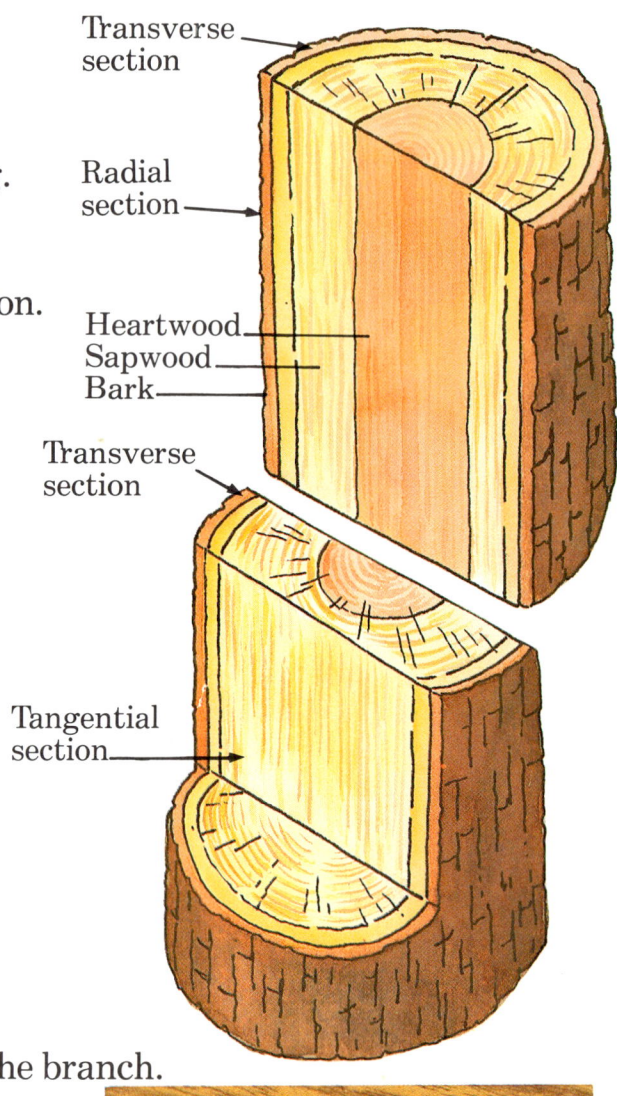

Timber from trees

Timber or wood is made in the trunk and larger branches of your tree. All wood is produced by a single ring of living cells called the cambium. The cambium cells form a cylinder just inside the inner bark.

The cambium cells divide to form cells on their *outside* called phloem. Phloem cells become layers which carry food around the tree.
As the cambium cells constantly form phloem, the older phloem layers are pushed outwards, become corky and die.
We see these layers as the outer bark. (see page 25)

Cambium cells divide and also form sapwood cells on their *inner* side called xylem.
The sapwood cells carry water from the roots to the leaves.
The cambium constantly divides, forming new sapwood. Older sapwood layers near the middle of the tree thicken and die.
We call these dead cells heartwood. Heartwood forms the strong central column of the tree.

Man uses sapwood and heartwood as timber. Freshly cut timber needs to dry out or season before it can be used.
Find out all you can about the price of timber. How much is your tree worth as timber?

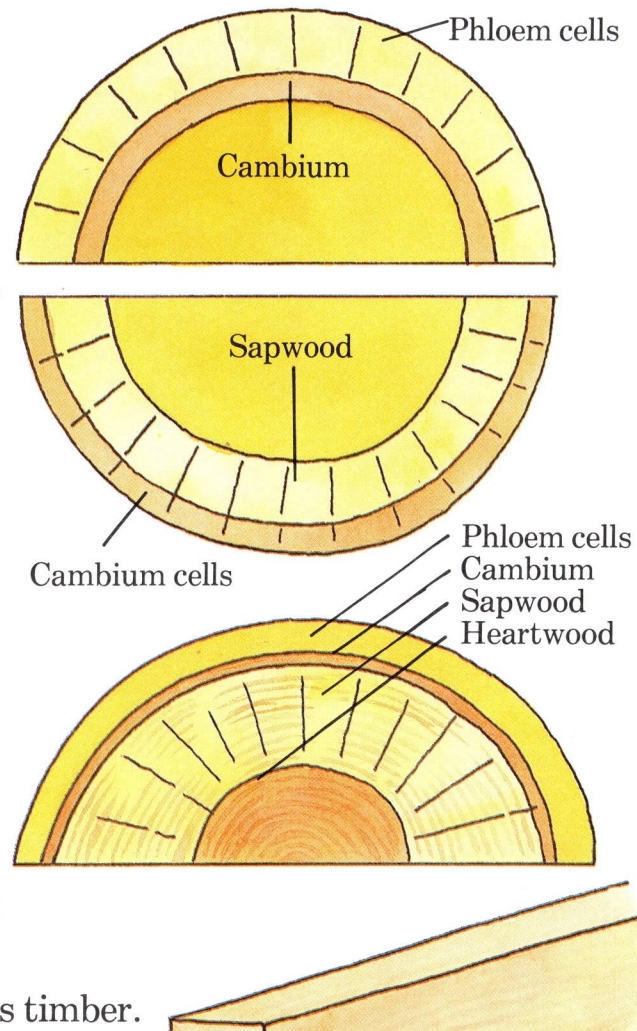

Chapter 5 Plants and animals on trees

Exploring leaf litter

Fallen leaves left on the ground become leaf litter.
Is there any leaf litter under your tree?
Find a tree with leaf litter under it.
Explore the leaf litter.
What colour are the leaves in the litter?
Are there any complete leaves in the litter?
Collect any leaf skeletons and use them to make patterns. (see page 15)

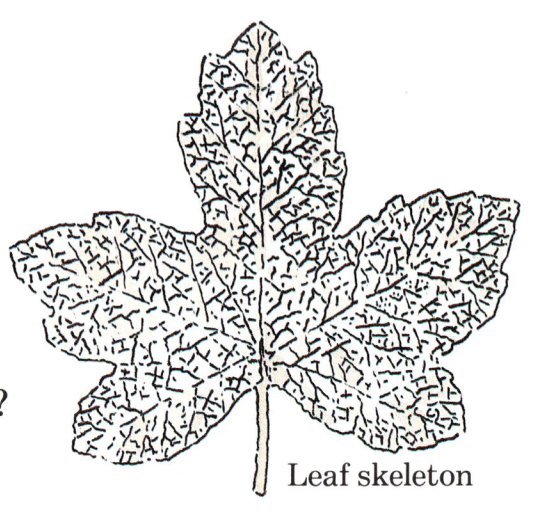
Leaf skeleton

Are there any pieces of twig in the leaf litter?
Are there tree fruits or seeds in the leaf litter?
Are any of them developing into young trees?
Are there fruits or seeds from other plants in the leaf litter?

Seedling

Use a spade to dig into the leaf litter.
How deep is the leaf litter?
Look at the bottom layers of the leaf litter.
Is this layer dry or damp?
Can you find any rotten pieces of twig?

Collect some leaf litter.
Place it in a plastic funnel.
Stand the funnel in a jar.
Place a lamp above the funnel.
Tiny animals will move away from the heat and light and drop into the jar.
Draw the animals that you find.
Try to identify these animals.

Plants growing under trees

When your tree has all its leaves, stand under it and look up at the sky. DO NOT LOOK DIRECTLY AT THE SUN AS IT WILL DAMAGE YOUR EYES.
How much of the sky is covered by your tree?
Look at the ground under your tree. How dark is the shadow of your tree?
Mark on the ground the extent of your tree's shadow.
Notice that the shadow varies with the time of day.

Are there plants growing in the shadow of your tree?
Are these plants different from the plants growing in the open?
How many different kinds of plants can you find growing in your tree's shadow?
Which plants grow closest to the trunk of your tree?
Are there tree seedlings growing in the shadow of your tree?

Compare the shadow of your tree with that of different trees.
Which trees cast the darkest shadows?
Why do these trees cast dark shadows?
What plants grow under these trees?

Shadow

Plants on trees

Which plants have you seen climbing trees?
Some climbing plants are poisonous, so check with an adult before going close to the tree.
How are the plants climbing the tree?
Where are the roots of the climbing plant?
Are the climbing plants damaging the tree?

Look closely at the trunk of your tree.
Are there any small moss plants growing on the trunk of your tree?
Do the moss plants grow all around the trunk?
Where does the rain run down the trunk? (see page 8)
Do mosses grow in damp places?

Are there lichens growing on the trunk of your tree?
Is there more than one kind of lichen growing on your tree?
Carefully remove a few moss and lichen plants from your tree.
Look at the plants through a hand lens. Draw what you see.
Find out about mosses and lichens.
Compare the mosses and lichens growing on your tree with any others that you can find.
Are there any other plants growing on your tree?

Lichens

Crusty lichen attached by entire under-surface

Leafy type attached by many root-like threads

Fruity type attached only at its base

Animals on trees

Do any mammals, other than humans, visit your tree?
What are the mammals doing in your tree?

Do birds visit your tree?
What are the birds doing in your tree?
Record all your bird observations.
Do birds nest in your tree?
Watch for nest building and keep a diary of the nest building activity.

Are there any insects flying around your tree? Watch for flies, mosquitoes, bees, wasps, butterflies and moths visiting your tree.
Find out all you can about these insect visitors.

Explore the trunk of your tree for small animals. Look into the cracks in the bark.
Use a small paint brush to put the small animals you find into a jar.
Use a lens to look at the animals.
Draw what you see.

If your tree has a low branch put a newspaper on the ground under the branch.
Hit the bark sharply with a strong stick.
Hit the branch where it is not likely to break.
Which small animals are knocked out of your tree?
Compare the small animals that you find in your tree with small animals found in other trees.
Which tree has the most small animals in it?
Does this tree have the most leaf damage?

Exploring rotten wood

Find a rotten log. Are there any plants growing on the log?
If there are any fungi growing on your log, be very careful, as many fungi are poisonous.
If you touch the fungi remember to wash your hands carefully and don't put your hands near your face.

Are there any holes in the bark? What do you think caused these holes?

Bracket fungi

Carefully roll the log over.
What can you find underneath your log?
Is it damp under the log?
Record the small animals that are under your log.

Use a large nail to lift off a piece of bark from your rotten log.
Are there any white threads of fungus under the bark?
Which small animals are under the bark?
Draw these animals.

Are there any holes in the rotten wood?
How many of these holes are homes for small animals?
Press into the rotten wood with your finger nail.
What does the rotten wood feel like?

Look for dead trees. Do not get close to them as branches or the tree could fall on you. They are very dangerous. Keep your distance. Can you see fungus on the tree? What do people do to prevent trees from rotting?

Look at outdoor wooden structures. What prevents this wood from rotting?